THE BEST EVER

KIDS'

BOOK OF LISTS

Eugenie Allen

AN AVON CAMELOT BOOK

THE BEST EVER KIDS' BOOK OF LISTS is an original publication of Avon Books. This work has never before appeared in book form.

AVON BOOKS
A division of
The Hearst Corporation
1350 Avenue of the Americas
New York, New York 10019

Copyright © 1991 by Cloverdale Press Inc.
Published by arrangement with Cloverdale Press
Library of Congress Catalog Card Number: 91-6652
ISBN: 0-380-76357-5
RL: 4.1

Library of Congress Cataloging-in-Publication Data:

Allen, Eugenie
  The best ever kids' book of lists/Eugenie Allen.
    p.   cm.—(An Avon Camelot book)
  Summary: Presents forty unusual lists with an emphasis on nature, from the ten grossest vegetables to ten natural phenomena involving the number ten.
  1. Handbooks, vade-mecums, etc.—Juvenile literature. 2. Curiosities and wonders—Juvenile literature. [1. Curiosities and wonders. 2. Natural history—Miscellanea.] I. Title.   91-6652
AG105.A256   1991   CIP
031.02—dc20   AC

First Avon Camelot Printing: August 1991

CAMELOT TRADEMARK REG. U.S. PAT. OFF. AND IN OTHER COUNTRIES, MARCA REGISTRADA, HECHO EN U.S.A.

Printed in the U.S.A.

OPM 10 9 8 7 6 5 4 3 2

Interior Illustrations: Harold Nolan, Robert Brown, Jennifer Bevill, and Christopher R. Neyen
Book design: Harold Nolan and Laura-Ann Robb

THE BEST EVER
KIDS'
BOOK OF LISTS

CONTENTS

REVOLTING EATING HABITS 1

REALLY REVOLTING EATING HABITS 4

HOP TO IT! Things That Jump 7

WORLD'S GREATEST DADS 10

CREATURES OF THE NIGHT. 13

INCREDIBLE JOURNEYS 14

FANTASTIC FLOATERS 18

NAME THAT THING 21

AMAZING ORIGINS OF EVERYDAY THINGS .22

NATURE'S MOST LETHAL WEAPONS. 24

GAGGLES, SMACKS, AND GAMS: The
    Strangest Names for Animal Groups 27

PARTNERS AND PALS 28

PEOPLE EAT THE STRANGEST THINGS 31

THE WORLD'S WORST NATURAL DISASTERS 32

GREAT PRETENDERS 34

THE LONELIEST ANIMALS 37

THINGS THAT GLOW IN THE DARK 39

JUST HANGIN' AROUND: Things That
Hang Upside Down 40

BEAUTY IS ONLY SKIN DEEP: The Ugliest
Animals 42

THE BIGGEST CROWDS 44

THE GROSSEST VEGETABLES 46

WHAT DO YOU GET WHEN YOU CROSS 48

MISTAKEN IDENTITY 50

GREAT DEFENSES 52

TOTALLY NATURAL WAYS TO MEASURE
TIME—WITHOUT A CLOCK OR
CALENDAR 54

LIFE AFTER DEATH: Things That Happen
After Plants and Animals Are Dead—
or Seem to Be! 57

CONTENTS

NOW YOU SEE IT, NOW YOU DON'T:
Things That Are Invisible to the Naked
Eye and How We See or Measure Them . 60

TINY CONQUERORS 62

GREAT SURVIVORS 64

THE LONGEST-LIVING THINGS ON EARTH . . 66

THAT'S INCREDIBLE! Amazing Things
That Happen in Nature 69

ANIMAL EXPRESSIONS 72

EYE SEE YOU! Amazing Types of Eyes 74

NATURE'S SPEED DEMONS: Look Out!
There They Went! 76

HAVE YOU EVER SEEN 80

HOME SWEET HOME: Places Where
Creatures Live 82

MODERN CREATURES THAT WERE HERE
WHEN DINOSAURS ROAMED THE
EARTH—OR BEFORE! 84

HEY BIG GUY: Enormous Living Things 87

ALL IN THE FAMILY: Strange Sets of
Relatives 90

THE SCARIEST PEOPLE EVER: Horrible
Humans in Fact and Fiction 93

BELIEVE IT OR NOT: Mythical Creatures—
or Are They? 96

**THE BIGGEST BEETLES, BUGS, AND
BUTTERFLIES** 99

FROM AARDVARK TO ZEBU: The
Strangest Names in Nature 102

THE WORLD'S LONGEST RIVERS 105

BRAVE NEW WORLDS—Famous Voyages
of Discovery 106

TEN NATURAL WONDERS OF THE WORLD .. 110

IT'S YOUR PLANET—Help Protect It! 112

NOW IT'S YOUR TURN: Make Up Some
Lists of Your Own! 116

INTRODUCTION

- What's the heaviest insect on Earth?
- What creatures have the most disgusting eating habits?
- What bird flies 11,000 miles every year?
- What's the most poisonous snake in the world?
- What animals are the loneliest?
- What were the world's worst natural disasters?

Give up? Don't—you'll find the answers to all these questions in the following pages, as well as hundreds of other fascinating facts about the world around us and the sky above. And you'll meet some of the most peculiar creatures in Mother Nature's vast family, like zonkeys, pangolins, water bears, and piddocks, not to mention mammals that lay eggs, plants that eat insects, and birds that can't fly. You'll discover trees that live 5,000 years, beans that hop, fish that glow in the dark, and much, much more.

So what are you waiting for? Start your incredible journey through the amazing world of nature in THE BEST EVER KIDS' BOOK OF LISTS!

REVOLTING
EATING HABITS

House mice eat just about anything that's waxy or fatty—soap, butter, candles—and of course, cheese.

Humans
eat raw oysters and clams that are still alive.

The starfish can stick its stomach out through its mouth to digest its food, usually oysters, clams, or mussels. And if it gets indigestion, the starfish simply gets rid of its upset stomach and grows a new one.

Right after it hatches, **the owl butterfly caterpillar** eats its own eggshell.

The anteater really *does* eat ants. It pokes a hole in an anthill, sticks its long tongue inside, sucks out the ants, and swallows them.

Some **ribbon worms** eat *themselves* if they can't find any other food! One worm ate 95% of its own body, but made an amazing recovery when it found some food it liked better.

The female black widow spider sometimes eats the male during or after mating.

2

Certain types of plants called **bromeliads,** which are relatives of the pineapple, catch water in their spike leaves to attract rainforest creatures like mosquitos, snails, flies, and ants. Then they digest this "animal soup" using special enzymes.

The alligator snapping turtle has a wiggly pink appendage in its mouth that looks just like a worm. When fish take the bait, the turtle snaps its killer jaws shut and gobbles up its prey.

A school of hungry **piranhas,** small but fierce tropical fish, can eat all the flesh off its prey in a matter of minutes, leaving only a skeleton!

REALLY
REVOLTING
EATING HABITS

- **Leeches** can consume five times their weight in blood at a single meal.

- The **Venus flytrap** is an insectivorous (insect-eating) plant that catches unlucky bugs between its hairy leaves and eats them alive, dissolving their bodies with special chemicals it produces.

- **Gila monsters** are lizards that eat enough at one meal to last for months, storing the leftovers in their tails!

- The **COW** keeps chewing, swallowing, and spitting up a lump of grass called a *cud* until the cud has traveled through the four compartments of its stomach and is fully digested.

- **Mother birds** mash up worms in their beaks, then spit out the mush to feed their babies.

- The **snapping turtle** eats fellow snappers without an ounce of guilt!

- The **black swallower fish** is only six inches long, but it eats whole fish that are twice its size. It uses the movable teeth in its throat to help shove food down to its stretchy stomach.

- The **boa constrictor** kills its prey—usually mice, rats, and birds—by coiling itself around its victim and squeezing it to death. Then it opens its hinged jaws wide enough to swallow it whole.

- **Vultures** eat rotting carcasses of almost any creature.

- **Earthworms** eat dirt.

(If your mother tells you it's disgusting when you chew with your mouth open, run some of *these* eating habits past her!)

HOP TO IT!
Things That Jump

- **Grasshoppers**

- **Popcorn**

- On May 18, 1986, a **bullfrog** named Rosie the Ribeter set a record at the annual Calaveras County Jumping Frog Jubilee in Angels Camp, California, by covering 21 feet, 5¾ inches in three consecutive leaps. Many years before that, the American author Mark Twain wrote a story called "The Celebrated Jumping Frog of Calaveras County" about this annual contest.

- **Dolphins** can't breathe underwater, so they jump out of the water every few minutes to get a breath of air.

- **Cats** are able to jump over six feet in the air from a standing start. That's more than seven times the height of an average cat standing on all fours!

- The **ground** during an earthquake.

- **MEXICAN JUMPING BEANS**

- **Rabbits**

- **People** jump out of airplanes, using parachutes that allow them to float safely to the ground.

- **Kangaroos** can jump higher than 10 feet, and farther than 44 feet.

Mexican jumping beans, also known as vest-pocket pets, have amazed and delighted people for centuries. What makes those little brown pellets hop around? To begin with, they're not really beans at all. They're tiny fruits that are inhabited by the caterpillar of a Central American butterfly. The caterpillar bores so deep inside the fruit that you can't see it from outside. When the "bean" is exposed to warmth, like the warmth of your hand as you hold it, it "jumps" as the caterpillar wakes up from its nap and moves around.

9

World's Greatest Dads

The males of many animal species mate with the females and then disappear. But some creatures, especially birds and amphibians, take fatherhood very seriously and help to care for their young both before and after they're born. The best example of a good father, of course, is the human father. More and more dads are helping moms through pregnancy and childbirth. They're also sharing the job of raising their children. Here are some other fathers that do their part.

- The **male seahorse** fertilizes the female's eggs and then carries them in a pouch on his belly until they are ready to hatch.

- **Male penguins** "babysit" by keeping the female's eggs warm while she takes a break.

- **Male swans** stay with one mate for life. They protect the mother swans and their young fiercely, attacking anyone or anything that threatens them.

- **Male catfish** carry the eggs of their offspring in their mouths for two months before the eggs hatch.

- **Male toadfish** guard their eggs, snapping ferociously at anyone who dares come near.

- The **male marmoset**, a type of monkey, cleans his offspring's fur after it is born and carries it around for the first few months of life.

- The **male malee fowl** helps build a nest for the female's eggs and stays close by while they incubate, adjusting leaves and sand to make sure the temperature stays at around 92° Fahrenheit.

- The **male midwife toad**'s responsibility is to balance the eggs he fertilizes on his hind legs and take them into the water every now and then to keep them moist!

- The **male rhea**, an ostrich-like bird, builds the nest, guards and hatches the eggs of its young, and protects the chicks from other animals. The dad drives the mother away and raises the chicks himself. He's a good father but a mean mate!

- The **male Darwin's frog** is only one inch long and lives in South America. He carries his young in long sacs in his throat until they hatch, turn into tadpoles, and lose their tails.

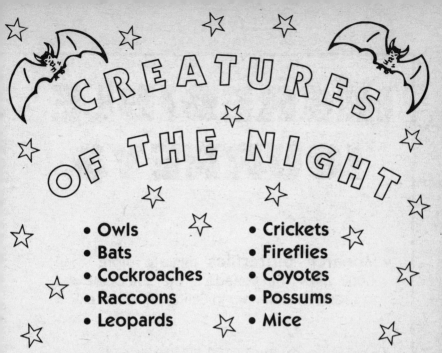

CREATURES OF THE NIGHT

- Owls
- Bats
- Cockroaches
- Raccoons
- Leopards
- Crickets
- Fireflies
- Coyotes
- Possums
- Mice

Creatures that do all or most of their business during the night are called *nocturnal*. Some prefer nighttime activity because the place where they live is too hot for them to do anything but sleep during the day. Others, like owls, come out at night because their eyesight is well adapted to seeing in the dark. Bats don't see very well at night, but they send out high-pitched squeaks that echo back from anything in their path. The bat uses these echoes to locate things in the dark, and to avoid obstacles. Creatures that sleep at night and feed by day are called *diurnal*. They include butterflies, monkeys, songbirds, lizards, honeybees, and humans—though if you have a baby brother or sister, you know that not *all* humans sleep all night!

INCREDIBLE JOURNEYS

- **Monarch butterflies** migrate more than 4,000 miles from Canada to the Gulf of Mexico to spend the summer in California and Mexico.

- The two **waterfalls** at Niagara Falls have "moved" 6 miles upstream in the past 10,000 years, because the force of tons of cascading water has worn away the stone beneath them.

- **Galapagos turtles** spend the rainy season at the ocean shore, then climb 2,000 feet up into the hills of the Galapagos Islands for the dry season.

- **Ash** from the 1980 volcanic eruption of Mount St. Helens in Washington traveled nearly 1,000 miles in just fifteen minutes! Within a month, the ash had made its way around the world—more than 20,000 miles.

- Certain **eels** travel more than 1,000 miles from their river homes in Europe and America to the Atlantic Ocean, where they mate and die. Their offspring are left to hatch alone and make the year-long trip back to where the parents came from, purely by instinct!

- **Baby shrimp** swim up to 100 miles in three weeks to get to the "nursery" where they will mature. A few months later, they return to their birthplace to mate.

- In 1979, a family in Texas lost some important **papers** in a tornado. The papers were discovered and returned to them by people from an Oklahoma town 150 miles away!

- For the past 200 million years, the Earth's great landmasses, called **CONTINENTS**, have been shifting at the rate of an inch or less each year.

- **Coconuts** that drop from trees growing on beaches often fall into the ocean and float thousands of miles to other tropical shores, where they sprout into new trees.

- Each June, a bird called the **Arctic tern** flies 11,000 miles from the Antarctic to the Arctic Circle, where it spends the summer.

Geologists have come up with a theory called *plate tectonics* to explain why the same kinds of fossils can be found on opposite sides of the world, and why the shorelines of northern Africa and southern Europe look as if they could fit together like the pieces of a jigsaw puzzle. There is strong evidence that the **continents** were once a single, giant landmass that geologists call Pangaea. But because the continents are like *plates* of rock and soil floating on the hot, molten core of the Earth, Pangaea began to separate, forming the continents as we know them today. In the past 180 million years, North America has drifted 5,000 miles west-northwest. And in your very own lifetime, the Atlantic Ocean will become wider by several feet.

What's the longest distance *you* have ever traveled?

FANTASTIC FLOATERS

- **Jellyfish**

- **Clouds**

- **ICEBERGS**

- **Volcanic rock**, called pumice, is filled with tiny air bubbles that make it lighter than water.

- **Balsa wood**

- When **dandelions** go to seed, their bright yellow flowers turn into puffy white seed heads. Attached to the top of each seed is a tuft of hairlike fibers that acts like a tiny parachute. When a breeze comes along, it carries the "parachute" and its seed to a new location.

Icebergs are huge mountains of freshwater ice that were once part of the great masses of ice called glaciers. Most of Greenland and Antarctica is covered by glaciers all year long, and glaciers also cover parts of Alaska. Along the coast, parts of the glaciers break off and fall into the sea, becoming icebergs. They are very dangerous to ships because most of the iceberg is hidden under the water. That means that when an iceberg is sighted from a ship, nobody can tell how big it really is. On April 14, 1912, the British ship *Titanic* hit an iceberg 500 miles south of Newfoundland and sank. More than 1,500 people lost their lives. The sinking of the *Titanic* is one of the greatest tragedies that ever took place at sea.

- Utah's Great Salt Lake is so salty that **people** who swim in it bob around like corks. That's because the density of the salt water is greater than that of a human body.
- **Ducks**
- There is so much **seaweed** floating in the Sargasso Sea, an area of the North Atlantic Ocean, that early navigators thought it was a series of islands inhabited by huge sea monsters lying in wait for their ships! The name "Sargasso" comes from "sargaço," a Portuguese word for seaweed.

NAME THAT THING!

Do you know the name for...

1. A seal, a walrus, or another animal who uses finlike flippers to get around?
2. A large, fierce, bearded baboon?
3. A toothless anteater whose body is covered with scales?
4. A 14-legged freshwater creature that lives in a shell?
5. A Chinese tree with fan-shaped leaves?
6. A type of grass that is used to make syrup or sweetener?
7. A rat-like pouched animal (marsupial) that lives in Australia?
8. An American rodent that swims?

NAMES

A. Ginkgo
B. Ostracod
C. Sorghum
D. Pinniped

E. Bandicoot
F. Pangolin
G. Mandrill
H. Coypu

(Answers: 1D, 2G, 3F, 4B, 5A, 6C, 7E, 8H)

AMAZING ORIGINS OF EVERYDAY THINGS

- **Nylon** is made out of coal, air, and water.

- **SILK** is woven from thread spun by the silk-worm, a caterpillar that is native to the Far East and eats nothing but mulberry leaves.

- **Glass** is made out of sand baked at very high temperatures.

- **Pearls** are formed inside oyster shells. They start out as tiny grains of sand and get bigger as the irritated oyster secretes layers of a hard, shimmering substance called *nacre* that protects the oyster from the scratchy sand.

- **Gelatin**, the stuff that makes foods like Jell-O both wobbly and firm, is made by boiling the skin, bones, and tissues of animals.

- Both **nail polish** and **gasoline** are made from petroleum.

People have been making **silk** fabric from the silkworm's thread for nearly 5,000 years. The thread comes from the silkworm's cocoon, which it spins around and around its body. Each cocoon contains about half a mile of unbroken thread, which is combined with the threads from other cocoons and woven into beautiful fabric. The first silk was woven in China, and the Chinese wanted to keep the procedure a secret. People caught smuggling the precious worms out of the country were put to death. But eventually the technique (and the worms) spread to the Middle East and Europe. Besides being beautiful, silk is the strongest of all natural fibers. A thread of silk is stronger than the same size thread of some kinds of steel!

- The first **chewing gum** came from the sap of a Mexican jungle tree called the sapodilla.

NATURE'S MOST LETHAL WEAPONS

- The deadly **death-puffer fish** is poisonous when eaten. It causes paralysis, nausea, vomiting, and convulsions, and 60% of its victims don't live to have another meal!

- The **Brazilian wandering spider** is the most poisonous spider of all.

- The most poisonous snake on Earth is the **sea snake**, which lives off the coast of Australia.

- The **stonefish** lives in the tropical waters of the Indo-Pacific and kills people who accidentally step on its poisonous spines.

- The most lethal venom in the world comes from the skin of the **golden dart-poison frog** of South America. South American Indians dip their darts in the poison to kill their enemies. A single adult frog carries enough venom to kill nearly 1,500 people!

- The most poisonous mushroom is the **death cap**, also known as the destroying angel. It sends those who eat it into fits of vomiting and delirium and kills 90% of them within 15 hours.

(Don't worry about the mushrooms your mom buys in the supermarket— you may not think they taste very good, but they're perfectly safe.)

- The leaves of the **hemlock plant** can kill people who eat them.

- The **Australian sea wasp**'s sting is so deadly that it can kill its victims within three minutes by making their hearts stop.

- The **black widow spider**, whose black body bears a distinctive red hourglass-shaped mark, makes the victims of its bites very ill with cramps, sweating, intense pain, difficulty in breathing, chills, and fever. That's the bad news. The *good* news is that the black widow's bite is fatal to humans only 4% of the time.

- The most dangerous snake on Earth is the **king cobra** of southeast Asia. Besides having very powerful venom, the king cobra is *huge*—up to 16 feet long. It delivers its poison by sinking its hollow fangs into its victims.

Gaggles, Smacks, and Gams:
The Strangest Names for Animal Groups

Over the centuries, some pretty peculiar names have been given to the families and groups of animals that do not live alone. Check these out!

A **gaggle** of **geese**

A **smack** of **jellyfish**

A **gam** of **whales**

An **exaltation** of **larks**

A **murder** of **crows**

A **troop** of **kangaroos**

A **paddling** of **ducks**

A **clowder** of **cats**

A **shrewdness** of **apes**

A **crash** of **rhinoceroses**

Can you make up some funny names for groups of people or things? (For example, "a giggle of girls," "a crumble of cookies," etc.)

PARTNERS AND PALS

- The **honeybee** lives on the nectar it gathers from **flowers**, and the flowers are able to reproduce because the bee spreads their pollen from blossom to blossom, fertilizing them.

- The **tickbird** and the **rhinoceros** don't hang out together because they like each other so much, but because the tickbird likes to eat the ticks buried in the rhino's thick hide, and the rhino is happy to get rid of the annoying pests.

- **Lichen**, a flowerless, mosslike plant that grows on bare rocks and tree stumps, is a combination of certain types of **algae** and **fungi**, neither of which could exist without the other. The algae use light to make food in a process called photosynthesis; the fungi absorb water.

- A **sea anemone**, which is a relative of the jellyfish, is often attached to the outside of a **hermit crab**'s shell. The crab carries the anemone around and shares bits of food; the anemone returns the favor by hiding the crab among its stinging tentacles and attacking any enemies that might come near.

- The brightly colored **clown fish** lives among the tentacles of a different type of **anemone**, cleaning the creature in exchange for protection and leftover food.

- **Aphids**, the tiny green or whitish insects you sometimes find in your garden or on household plants, often live with **ants**. The aphids produce a sugary liquid called "honeydew" that the ants enjoy, and the ants carry the aphids from plant to plant so they can feed and keep producing honeydew.

- The **dog** is often called man's best friend, but **man** is a pretty good friend to the dog, too, giving it food and shelter in return for companionship and sometimes protection.

- Certain **bacteria** live in the roots of **legumes** like peas and beans, producing the nitrogen the plants need to survive in exchange for some food and a safe home.

- Other **bacteria** live inside plant-eating animals like **cows** and help them digest cellulose, a tough, woody material found in many plants.

- The deadly **Portuguese man-of-war jelly-fish** allows the tiny **man-of-war** fish to live among its poisonous tentacles, feeding on leftovers. In exchange, the little fish lures larger prey to an unexpected death.

When two different kinds of living things help each other, it's called *symbiosis,* which means "living together." Symbiosis can occur between two plants, two animals, or a plant and an animal. Sometimes, however, an organism called a *parasite* harms its plant or animal host. Fleas, ticks, and lice are all parasites. One of the biggest parasite plants is the *strangler fig*. It sprouts in a crevice high up in its host tree, wrapping the tree in dangling roots and leafy branches. The unfortunate tree eventually dies from a lack of sunlight. But the strangler fig isn't *all* bad. Its leaves and roots provide a home for many forest creatures that fertilize the soil beneath it when they die and fall to the forest floor. Their bodies decompose and fertilize the soil so other plants can flourish.

PEOPLE EAT THE STRANGEST THINGS!

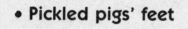

- **Pickled pigs' feet**
- **Tripe** (the inside of a cow's stomach)
- **Tongue**
- **Brains**
- **Oxtails**
- **Bird's nest soup**
- **100-year-old eggs**
- **Chocolate-covered ants**
- **Eels**
- **Octopus**
- **Caviar** (tiny, salty, *very expensive* fish eggs)
- **Sweetbreads** (the thymus glands of calves)

THE WORLD'S WORST NATURAL DISASTERS

Year	Disaster	Location	Death Toll
1201	earthquake	Near East and Mediterranean	1.1 million
1556	earthquake	China	830,000
1737	earthquake	India	300,000
1769–70	drought	India	up to 10 million
1865–66	drought	India	10 million
1877	flood	China	900,000
1881	cyclone	Indonesia	300,000
1923	earthquake	Japan	200,000
1970	cyclone	Bangladesh	500,000
1976	earthquake	China	242,000

The 1883 eruption of *Krakatoa*, a volcanic island in Indonesia, was probably the biggest natural explosion ever. The volcano hadn't erupted for about 200 years. Then suddenly it exploded with four huge bangs! More than half the island—4.3 cubic miles of earth—was shot as high as 34 miles and as far as 3,300 miles, and the sound was heard over 1/13th of the globe. Some say it was the loudest noise ever made on Earth! The eruption caused huge tidal waves, called tsunamis, that killed 36,000 people. Other natural disasters have had higher death tolls, but Krakatoa was remarkable because most of the people who died didn't even live on the island. Today, a new volcano called Anak Krakatoa (Child of Krakatoa) is rising out of the old one. Fortunately, we now have the technology to predict and measure volcanic eruptions, so far fewer people die as a result of such catastrophes.

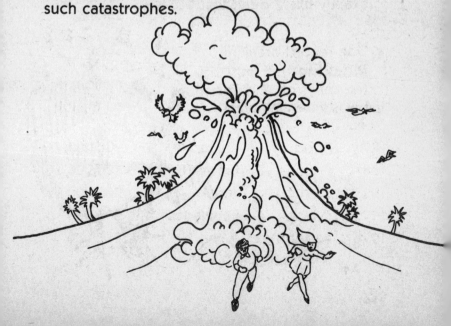

GREAT PRETENDERS

- **Possums** play dead so their enemies will leave them alone.

- The fur of **arctic foxes** turns white in winter so they can blend in with the snow and hide from other animals (and men) who want to kill them.

- When it folds its wings and perches on a branch, the **Indian leaf butterfly** looks exactly like a dead leaf.

- One record-breaking **mockingbird** imitated the songs of 32 different birds in ten minutes!

- The caterpillars of some **swallowtail butter-flies** pass for bird droppings, so their enemies gladly pass them by.

- The **thorn shield bug** looks just like a thorn on a plant.

- The **sea urchin**, a spiny, round relative of the starfish, picks up pebbles, shells, and seaweed until it looks like part of the ocean floor.

- A fish called the **Nassau grouper** can change the pattern of its scales eight times in the space of a few minutes to blend in with the brightly colored coral on the sea floor where it lives.

- A beautiful, glittering metal known as **pyrite** looks like gold, but it doesn't act like it. Pyrite, also called "fool's gold," rusts when exposed to air and water.

- A **MIRAGE** might look like a puddle of water in the road, or a lake in the middle of the desert, but it's really nothing but a trick of light.

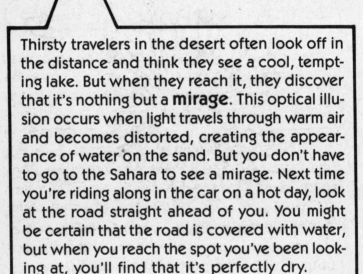

Thirsty travelers in the desert often look off in the distance and think they see a cool, tempting lake. But when they reach it, they discover that it's nothing but a **mirage**. This optical illusion occurs when light travels through warm air and becomes distorted, creating the appearance of water on the sand. But you don't have to go to the Sahara to see a mirage. Next time you're riding along in the car on a hot day, look at the road straight ahead of you. You might be certain that the road is covered with water, but when you reach the spot you've been looking at, you'll find that it's perfectly dry.

Can you think of some other things that aren't what they seem?

THE LONELIEST ANIMALS

In their natural state, most animals live in families or groups. But plenty of animals are solitary creatures. Some of them don't socialize because they inhabit shells or nests with room for just one occupant. Others have no family ties because they are able to provide only enough food for themselves. Here are some animals that live alone as adults, getting together with other members of their species only to mate or, in some cases, to raise their young.

- **Clams**

- **Bears**

- **Leopards**

- **Hermit crabs** live in the empty shells of other sea creatures and close them tightly against all intruders.

- **Chipmunks** live in burrows that they leave only to search for food.

- **Woodpeckers**

- **Human hermits** are people who, for one reason or another, choose to live by themselves, far away from others.

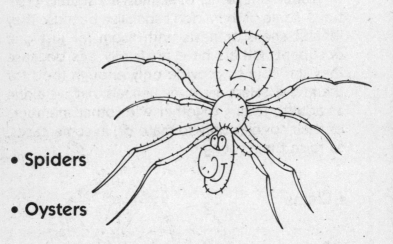

- **Spiders**

- **Oysters**

- **Orangutans** like to live by themselves in trees and rarely come down to the ground.

THINGS THAT GLOW IN THE DARK

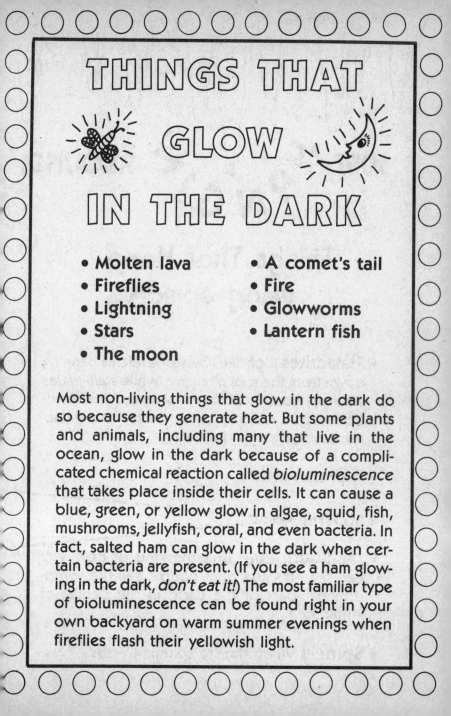

- Molten lava
- Fireflies
- Lightning
- Stars
- The moon
- A comet's tail
- Fire
- Glowworms
- Lantern fish

Most non-living things that glow in the dark do so because they generate heat. But some plants and animals, including many that live in the ocean, glow in the dark because of a complicated chemical reaction called *bioluminescence* that takes place inside their cells. It can cause a blue, green, or yellow glow in algae, squid, fish, mushrooms, jellyfish, coral, and even bacteria. In fact, salted ham can glow in the dark when certain bacteria are present. (If you see a ham glowing in the dark, *don't eat it!*) The most familiar type of bioluminescence can be found right in your own backyard on warm summer evenings when fireflies flash their yellowish light.

JUST HANGIN' AROUND:

Things That Hang
Upside Down

- **Stalactites** look like limestone icicles hanging down from the roof of a cave, while *stalagmites* stick up from the floor of a cave. (To remember which is which, just tell yourself that stalactites *stick tight* to the roof!)

- **Trapeze artists**

- **SLOTHS**

- The **South Pole** isn't the kind of pole you can see—it's just what people call the southernmost part of the Earth in the center of Antarctica.

- **Spiders** when they're spinning webs.

- **Butterflies** in the chrysalis stage.

- **Monkeys**

- **Bats**

- **Icicles**

- **Possums**

Sloths are South American animals that have a very peculiar way of moving around. They walk upside down, hanging from the branches of trees, and they almost never come down to the ground. There are two main types of sloths. One, called the *unau*, has two toes on its front feet. The other, called the *ai*, has three toes on its front feet. No matter how many toes it has, the sloth can dig its hooklike claws into the tree branches so securely that it even falls asleep upside down! Sloths sleep all day and move very, v-e-r-y slowly (about ⅓ of a mile an hour) at night. If somebody calls you "slothful," it's *not* a compliment. It means you're lazy and don't move very fast!

BEAUTY IS ONLY SKIN DEEP: The Ugliest Animals

- Manatee

- Tarantula

- Bullfrog

- Hatchetfish

- Platypus

- Vulture

- Slug

- Hyena

These creatures certainly wouldn't win any prizes in a beauty contest. But looks aren't everything, and some people are actually fond enough of some really ugly animals to keep them as pets. The *hairless cat*, for example, isn't soft and cuddly like its furry cousins, but people who are allergic and love cats anyway find the hairless variety better than no cat at all. The *gecko* is a weird-looking lizard with suction cups on its toes that enable it to walk up walls and across ceilings. People like geckos for pets because the lizards eat cockroaches and other insects that are sometimes found in houses and apartments. *Pit bulls* aren't related to cows—they're powerful dogs with a reputation for having an ugly disposition and attacking people. But pit bull owners insist that their pets are just as affectionate and loyal as other dogs.

- Iguana
- Kiwi bird
- Horned toad
- Hammerhead shark
- Blind cave fish
- Wild boar

THE BIGGEST CROWDS

- A single pair of mice can live to see 500,000 descendents.

- The sunfish carries 300 million eggs.

- There are anywhere from 1 million to 10 million insect species.

- A one-inch line on this page contains 100 million atoms.

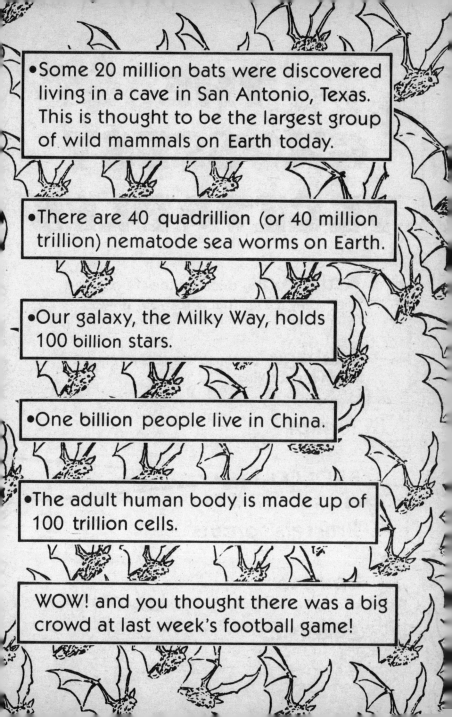

- Some 20 million bats were discovered living in a cave in San Antonio, Texas. This is thought to be the largest group of wild mammals on Earth today.

- There are 40 quadrillion (or 40 million trillion) nematode sea worms on Earth.

- Our galaxy, the Milky Way, holds 100 billion stars.

- One billion people live in China.

- The adult human body is made up of 100 trillion cells.

WOW! and you thought there was a big crowd at last week's football game!

THE GROSSEST VEGETABLES

Artichokes, because they're covered with spiny leaves that prick your fingers.

Cabbage, because it smells funny when it's cooking.

Turnips

BROCCOLI

Brussels sprouts

Spinach

Eggplant

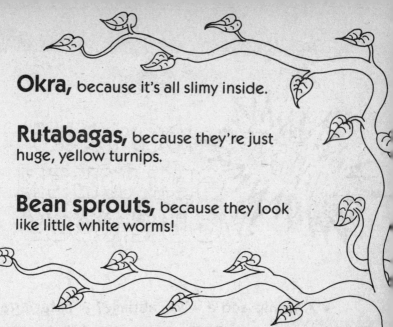

Okra, because it's all slimy inside.

Rutabagas, because they're just huge, yellow turnips.

Bean sprouts, because they look like little white worms!

President George Bush made national news when he banned **broccoli** from the dining table at the White House. "I do not like broccoli," he told reporters, "and I haven't liked it since I was a little kid and my mother made me eat it. I'm President of the United States and I'm not going to eat any more broccoli!" But First Lady Barbara Bush, who loves the green vegetable, didn't think American children should boycott broccoli, too. "He ate broccoli until he was 60," she pointed out to the reporters. "Tell them to eat it until *they're* 60!" (Meanwhile, the President continues to snack on pork rinds and ice cream.)

WHAT DO YOU GET WHEN YOU CROSS...

- A turnip and a wild cabbage? A **rutabaga.**

- A female horse and a male donkey? A **mule.**

- A female donkey and a male horse? A **hinny.**

- A tangerine and a grapefruit? A **tangelo.**

- A female lion and a male tiger? A **liger.**

- A male lion and a female tiger? A **tigon.**

- A donkey and a zebra? A **zonkey.**

- A woman and a fish? A **mermaid.**

All but one of the strange things on this list is a *hybrid*, a new type of plant or animal created when two different species of plants or animals mate, either by accident or with a little help from scientists. Hybrids have characteristics of both of their parents, but they're not exactly like either one. A mule, for instance, is about the same size as its mother, but it has a short head, long ears, and a short mane like its father. There's no such thing as a mother mule or a father mule—mules are sterile, which means that they can't reproduce.

Which one on this list is not a hybrid? HINT: Human beings only breed with each other, creating all sorts of interesting combinations, but certainly nothing with scales and fins.

MISTAKEN IDENTITY!

- The cuddly **koala bear** isn't really a bear at all. It's a *marsupial*, a type of mammal that carries its young in a pouch on its belly after they're born. Kangaroos and possums are also marsupials.

- **White ants** aren't ants, but termites, which are more closely related to roaches.

- **Sow bugs** (often called roly-polys) aren't bugs; they're *crustaceans*, which makes them relatives of lobsters and shrimp.

- **"Daddy longlegs"** aren't spiders; they're eight-legged *arthropods*, which don't have the web-spinning ability that spiders have.

- The **groundhog** is closely related to the rat, not the hog!

- A **moonrat** is not a rat; it's a member of the hedgehog family.

- A **Congo eel** isn't an eel; it's a lizard with four very small feet.

- The **guinea pig** is certainly not a pig; it's a rodent.

- **Scurvy grass** isn't grass, but a type of cabbage.

With so many plants and animals on Earth, it's easy to see why people get confused. Sometimes an animal is named by natives or by an explorer before biologists have studied it. For instance, the *capybara*, the world's largest rodent, is considered a *fish* in its native Venezuela because it spends a lot of time in the water. But habitat isn't everything. When classifying a living thing, biologists also consider things like mating habits, diet, even teeth! For example, by examining the hooves of the tiny *hyrax*, an African mammal, scientists learned that, even though it looks like an overweight guinea pig, it's really a distant cousin of the elephant.

Scientists name plants and animals in a seven-tiered classification system that describes everything from the *kingdom* (the most general category) all the way down to the *genus* and *species*, the plant or animal's scientific two-word name.

FACT: The scientific name for humans is *Homo sapiens*, which means "wise (or thinking) man." But did you know that our kingdom is *animalia*?

GREAT DEFENSES

- The **bombardier beetle** squirts harmful chemicals from its abdomen which explode like a bomb with a popping sound and a puff of smoke when they touch the air.

- The **Mexican horned toad** squirts blood from its eyes when threatened.

- The **octopus** shoots "ink"—which comes from its intestines—at its enemies, startling them and hiding the eight-legged creature so it can escape.

- **Skunks**, which are notorious for their foul-smelling spray, aim it at any animal—or human—who comes too close.

- The **Porcupine puffer fish** inflates itself into a prickly sphere so its enemies can't possibly swallow it.

- The **pink fairy armadillo** digs a hole, then squeezes into the hole head first, with only its rear end exposed. Fortunately its entire body is covered with armor!

- The **hedgehog** rolls itself into a spiny ball to protect its soft underside from predators like foxes.

- If an enemy grabs one of a **crab**'s eight legs, the crab simply detaches itself from its captive limb and scuttles away on the remaining seven!

- The **skink**, a common lizard, breaks off a piece of its tail when it's threatened. The tail wiggles about and distracts the enemy while the rest of the skink escapes!

- **Porcupines** run backwards and pierce their enemies' skin with their sharp quills. In one case, a porcupine killed a panther by piercing its head with 17 quills, two of which penetrated the panther's brain.

TOTALLY

NATURAL WAYS

TO MEASURE TIME—
Without a Clock or Calendar

- Roughly every 12 hours, the **ocean's tides** come in or go out. The water's gradual rising and falling is caused by regular changes in the pull of gravity between the moon and Earth.

- The **fiddler crab** changes its colors in 12-hour cycles, growing pale by night and dark by day.

- About every three months, the Earth's angle shifts as it spins on its axis and orbits the sun. These shifts cause the temperature and the amount of sunlight to change. These changes cause the **four seasons**, and they are most dramatic in the world's *temperate zones*, which are between 23½° and 66½° latitude north and south of the equator. Most of our continent of North America is in a temperate zone.

- The **Earth orbits the sun** in one year, or 365 days.

- **Lemmings**, tiny mammals that live on the Arctic tundra, go through three-year population explosions and then most of them die out every fourth year.

- Each year, **a tree adds another ring to its trunk**. So to find out how old a tree was at the time it was cut down, just count the rings. You can also tell what the weather was in any given year—in dry years, the rings are narrow because the tree didn't grow much; in wet years, the rings are wide.

- **Cicadas** hatch every 13 or 17 years, depending on the species. They spend more time as larvae than any other insect, but they only live about six weeks as adults. These periodical cicadas eat every leaf in sight, mate, lay eggs, and then die before the summer is over.

- Every 11 years, **sunspots**—dark, cool spots on the surface of the sun—show up in as many as a dozen different areas of the sun at once. But during the lulls in the sunspot cycle, there may not be a single visible sunspot.

- Every 76 years, **Halley's Comet** comes into view. It orbits the sun just as the nine planets in our solar system do. But one sun-orbiting "year" for Halley's comet is more than 75 years on Earth, so most of the time it's out of sight.

LIFE AFTER DEATH:
Things That Happen After Plants And Animals Are Dead— or Seem to Be!

- **Jellyfish** can sting even after they've died and have washed up on the beach.

- When the **water bear**, a microscopic eight-legged creature, becomes completely dried out, it reaches a point where its life is suspended. But it can "come back to life" when it gets wet, even 100 years later! Water bears can also survive very hot or very cold temperatures by going into this state of suspended animation.

- Remember the **dormouse** in *Alice in Wonderland*? When it hibernates, a curled-up dormouse seems to be dead. It can be removed from its nest and rolled around like a ball without waking up!

- The **earthworm** separates into two parts when an enemy picks it up, and even though one half may be eaten, the other half can still wiggle safely away.

- The **creosote bush**, a desert plant, drops its leaves and seems dead in dry weather. When it rains, though, the bush comes back to life.

- **Dead people**'s hair and nails appear to continue to grow because their skin shrivels up after they die.

- **Hummingbirds** have to flap their tiny wings so fast and eat so much during the day that at night they fall into a deep sleep called torpidity, from which they can't be awakened.

- When the **ground squirrel** falls into a deep sleep, called *hibernation*, beneath the Arctic tundra, its pulse drops from 200 beats per minute to 10 or less. **Bears** hibernate, too. They eat a lot and build up a layer of fat several weeks before winter begins. When the weather turns cold, it triggers a bear's instinct to hibernate. In this suspended state, it can live until spring on its own fat.

- **Snails** sometimes come out of their shells ready for a hearty meal after years of seeming to be dead.

- The **tuatara**, a reptile that hasn't changed much in the past 180 million years, is so sluggish that observers often think it's dead. It breathes once every seven minutes, and sometimes it even falls asleep in the middle of a meal.

NOW YOU SEE IT, NOW YOU DON'T:

Things That Are Invisible to the Naked Eye and How We See or Measure Them

- **Bacteria** are enlarged by a **microscope**.

- **Distant stars** are brought into view by a **telescope**.

- **Temperature** is measured by a **thermometer**.

- **Speed** is gauged by a **speedometer**.

- **Wind** is measured by an **anemometer**.

- **Electricity** is measured by a **voltameter**.

- **Odors** are detected by our **noses**.

• **Time** is kept by a **clock.**

We use thermometers to measure **tempera-ture**—how hot or cold something is. The most common type of thermometer—the kind you stick in your mouth to find out whether you have a fever—is a thin glass tube containing mercury, a metallic element that expands when it is heated making it rise up the tube. The normal human temperature is 98.6° Fahrenheit; a life-threatening fever is 106° Fahrenheit. (The Fahrenheit scale is one of three different scales used for measuring temperature. The others are the Celsius scale and the Kelvin scale. Fahrenheit is abbreviated "F.")

The temperature of the surface of the sun is about 11,000° F, while the clouds of the planet Pluto have an average temperature of 400° F *below zero*! Naturally, scientists can't take the temperature of the sun or the planets with the kind of thermometers used on humans. So they use special devices called *pyrometers*, which measure the amount of infrared radiation, a type of heat, produced by faraway objects.

• **Sound** is registered by our **ears.**

TINY CONQUERORS

- **Shrews**, tiny animals that weigh less than one ounce, have to eat every two hours. They are so fierce that they sometimes attack and eat animals many times their size.

- The eight-inch **tiger salamander** is almost as fierce as the shrew when it comes to food; it can swallow grasshoppers, spiders, worms, and even mice in a single bite!

- The **date mussel**, a mollusk that lives in the Mediterranean, can bury itself deep in limestone by dissolving the soft rock with powerful chemicals from its body.

- The **piddock**, another type of mollusk, actually drills holes in solid rock by twisting its sharp shell. The piddock draws food and oxygen through one of its two body tubes, and excretes waste and tiny pieces of drilled rock through the other tube.

- **Termites** can ruin an entire house by eating away at the wood.

- **Mosquitoes** annoy us every summer with their itchy, painful bites. In some tropical climates, mosquitoes do even more harm. They carry and spread bacteria that cause diseases like malaria and yellow fever.

- Even though they're completely blind, carnivorous **army ants** march through tropical forests in columns of up to 20 million, eating every insect in sight. They will even attack large animals and humans, though they aren't usually able to kill them.

- **Fleas** can turn even the fiercest dog into a whining, scratching pup.

- **Rats**, among the most despised creatures on Earth, have literally changed the course of history. In the 1300s an outbreak of a plague called the Black Death killed three-fourths of the population of Europe and Asia. The plague was spread by fleas from infected rats. Today, rats outnumber people in North America, and they thrive in places like sewers and subways.

- Bloodsucking **African tsetse flies** spread African sleeping sickness to the humans they bite, and infect animals with disease as well.

GREAT SURVIVORS

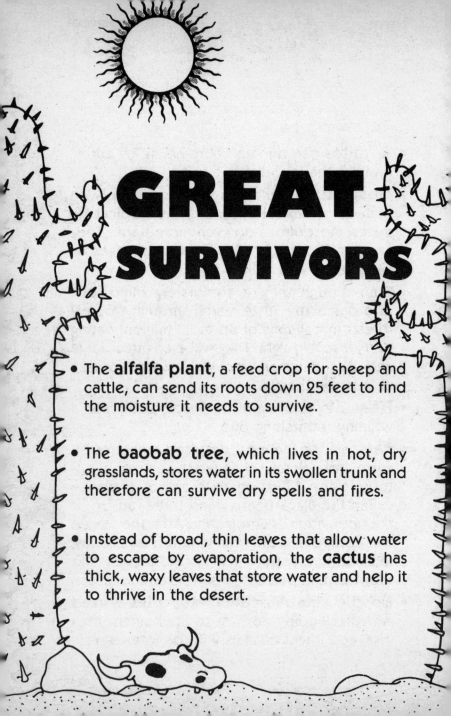

- The **alfalfa plant**, a feed crop for sheep and cattle, can send its roots down 25 feet to find the moisture it needs to survive.

- The **baobab tree**, which lives in hot, dry grasslands, stores water in its swollen trunk and therefore can survive dry spells and fires.

- Instead of broad, thin leaves that allow water to escape by evaporation, the **cactus** has thick, waxy leaves that store water and help it to thrive in the desert.

- **Camels** are perfectly suited to desert life. They can travel for up to seven days in broiling heat without water, and then they drink nearly 30 gallons of water in ten minutes to replenish their bodies. In the winter, camels can get all the water they need from eating plants.

- The **dwarf willow**, which grows in the Arctic Circle, stays close to the cold ground, growing only four inches high but spreading its branches out as far as ten feet to soak up what little water there is.

- The **desert bighorn ram** can go for days without water and scales rocky cliffs easily, outrunning even mountain lions.

- **Polar bears** spend the summer and fall eating lots of meat, and then spend the winter and spring living off the fat stored in their bodies.

- **Seals** are pretty tough cookies. Seals that live in cold climates have a thick layer of insulating blubber. One variety, the Weddell seal, can break airholes in the ice with its teeth.

THE LONGEST-LIVING THINGS ON EARTH

- **Tortoises** trudge around the earth for up to 150 years.

- **Bristlecone pine trees** can live for 5,000 years.

- **Oak trees** live for up to 800 years.

- Some **HUMANS** have lived to be 120 years old.

- **Whales** can keep spouting for 80 years.

- **Sequoias**, also known as Sierra redwoods, can live for more than 4,000 years. They grow only on the western slopes of California's Sierra Nevada Mountains. The General Sherman, a giant sequoia in Sequoia National Park, compares in age with the ancient pyramids of Egypt. It may be as many as 3,500 years old!

Humans have always wanted to live forever, but they've never wanted to *look* as if they've lived forever! For hundreds of years, explorers searched for the mythical Fountain of Youth, which supposedly restored youth to those who drank from it. In the Middle Ages, many people died before the age of thirty, and few people lived to be much older than fifty; today, thanks to improvements in our diet and the elimination of many diseases, we Americans can expect to live for about 75 years, and some people live to be well over 100. The oldest confirmed age for a human is 120, though claims have been made of people living to the ripe old age of 256!

- The **box turtle** can hang in there for 60 years or more.

- **Chimpanzees** keep swinging for 40 years.

- The **eagle owl** knows who's who for 65 years.

- **Elephants** remember a lifetime of 80 years.

It's said that if you multiply the age of a cat, dog, or horse by seven, you'll find out how old the animal is in human years. For example, a five-year-old cat would be thirty-five in human terms. If you have any pets, how old would they be if they were people?

THAT'S INCREDIBLE!

Amazing Things That Happen in Nature

- **Ostriches** are birds but they can't fly. Ostriches are so big that one ostrich egg would make as many omelets as two dozen eggs from a hen!

- The **mudskipper** is a fish, but it can breathe air and walk on its front fins.

- **Rat snakes** can climb trees by flattening themselves and wedging their flat sides into cracks in the bark.

- A bush can tell you the temperature outside. On a warm summer day, the leaves of the **rhododendron** stick straight out, but the colder it gets, the lower they droop, until they hang straight down when it's zero degrees Fahrenheit.

- During a total solar **ECLIPSE**, the sun is hidden from view by the moon for several minutes and the daytime sky becomes as dark as night.

- All **earthworms** are *hermaphrodites*, meaning that they're both male and female.

- The **electric ray**, which lives in the Atlantic Ocean and grows to be five feet long, can electrocute its prey. It stuns small fish with a 220-volt shock before eating them.

- **Platypuses** have bills and lay eggs like ducks, but they're *mammals* like cats and dogs.

FACT: The "mammal club" has members of all shapes and sizes, from the two-inch shrew to the huge blue whale. There are over 5,000 species of mammals, and they all have four characteristics in common: They are all *vertebrates* (that is, they have backbones); they are all warm-blooded; they all have four-chambered hearts; and the females have glands that produce milk for feeding their young.

Every year or so, a total **eclipse** of the sun is visible somewhere in the world. If you've ever seen a total eclipse, you know how awesome it is. But *never* look directly at the sun during an eclipse. Even if you can't see the sun, its rays are still powerful enough to damage your eyes or even blind you! In ancient times, people thought that a solar eclipse meant something terrible was going to happen. Now astronomers can predict when an eclipse will occur, and scientists travel across the globe to observe it from the best angle. Using special instruments, they can see the sun's *corona*, a beautiful whitish halo of gases, and its *prominences*, streams of glowing hot hydrogen that flow out into space. By studying our sun, which is really a star, scientists hope to learn more about other stars in our galaxy. Maybe one day they will find out that some of those stars support life on other planets, the way the sun does on Earth!

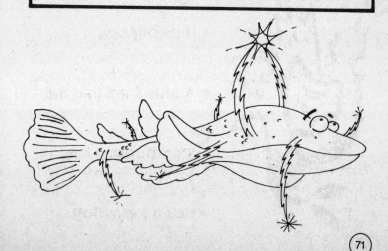

ANIMAL EXPRESSIONS

- I'm hungry as a **bear**.

- Don't **chicken** out.

- **Cat** got your tongue?

- She's as quiet as a **clam**.

- Stop **horsing** around!

- Let's **pig** out.

- A little **bird** told me.

- Stop **bug**ging him.

- He's a lucky **dog**.

- Don't be so **crab**by.

- He looks a little **sheep**ish.

- You're not going to **weasel** out of this!

- She has a memory like an **elephant**.

- I'll wait for you till the **cows** come home.

Can you think of some more expressions like these?

EYE SEE YOU!
Amazing Types of Eyes

- The **anableps**, a tropical fish, has four eyes. One pair looks at things underwater; the other pair looks at things above water.

- The biggest eyes in the world belong to the **giant squid**, whose eyes are up to fifteen inches across.

- The **rhinocerous iguana** of Puerto Rico has three eyes.

- The **flatfish turbot** starts life with two eyes, one on each side of its head. But one eye eventually moves so that the fish ends up with both eyes on the top of its head!

- The **eagle** has telescopic vision that enables it to see its prey from three miles away.

- Instead of eyes, the **earthworm** has light-sensitive spots up and down its back.

- The **copepod**, a tiny crustacean related to shrimps and crabs, has just one eye in the middle of its forehead, between its two feelers that are called antennae.

- A **chameleon**'s two eyes swivel independently so it can see in all directions—sometimes even forwards and backwards at the same time!

- The **Cyclops**, a creature from Greek mythology, has one huge eye in the middle of his forehead.

- A **housefly** has three simple eyes, which see things only dimly, and two huge *compound eyes* with a total of 8,000 light-sensitive cells. Each cell forms a portion of an image, refracting the image to create the effect of looking through a kaleidoscope.

Have you ever looked through a *kaleidoscope*? It's a two-part tube that has tiny pieces of colored glass in one section. When you turn that section, you can marvel at the many beautiful designs that are formed. That's something like what a fly sees!

NATURE'S SPEED DEMONS:

Look Out!

- **Dragonflies** are known as the fastest insect because they can zoom along at 60 miles an hour.

- **Black mambas**, the fastest snakes on earth, can move at the rate of 12 miles an hour.

- **Olympic athletes** who run the 100-meter race reach a speed of 26.32 miles an hour.

- The **killer whale** lumbers along at 30 miles an hour.

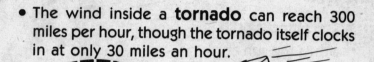

- The wind inside a **tornado** can reach 300 miles per hour, though the tornado itself clocks in at only 30 miles an hour.

- **Peregrine falcons** are the fastest bird, reaching a speed of 200 miles an hour when they dive.

- **Cheetahs** are the fastest four-legged animals, reaching 60 miles an hour at a clip.

There They Went!

- **Tsunamis**, the terrible tidal waves caused by earthquakes and volcanoes, can move at a rate of 490 miles an hour.

- The planet **Earth** orbits the sun at 66,641 miles an hour.

- **LIGHT** travels at 186,000 miles per second, or 670,600,000 miles an hour, or 6 trillion miles a year!

FACT: On the slow side, snails move just 10 to 12 feet per hour. But the bamboo plant, which can grow as much as 36 inches in one day, is pretty speedy for a plant!

How fast can you run? Have you ever clocked your speed?

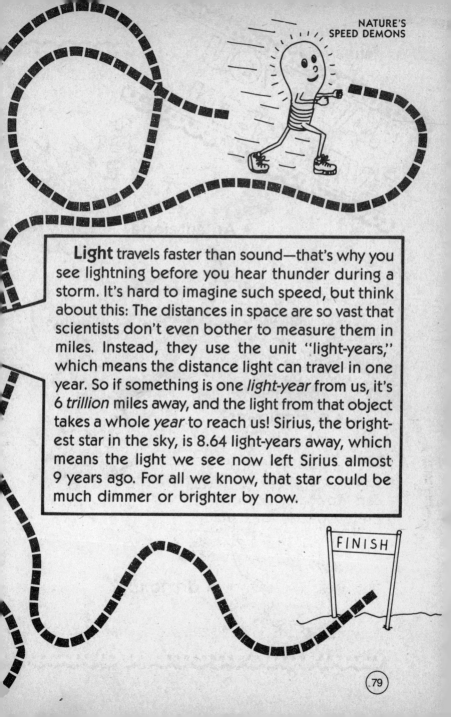

Light travels faster than sound—that's why you see lightning before you hear thunder during a storm. It's hard to imagine such speed, but think about this: The distances in space are so vast that scientists don't even bother to measure them in miles. Instead, they use the unit "light-years," which means the distance light can travel in one year. So if something is one *light-year* from us, it's 6 *trillion* miles away, and the light from that object takes a whole *year* to reach us! Sirius, the brightest star in the sky, is 8.64 light-years away, which means the light we see now left Sirius almost 9 years ago. For all we know, that star could be much dimmer or brighter by now.

FINISH

HAVE YOU EVER SEEN...

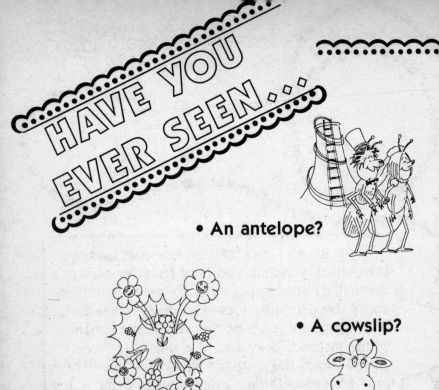

• An antelope?

• A cowslip?

• A sunflower?

• A dragonfly?

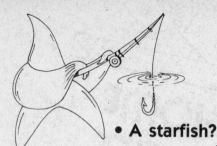

• A starfish?

• A horsefly?

• Milkweed?

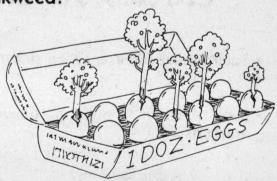

• An eggplant?

Places Where Creatures Live

- Squirrels live in nests called **dreys**.

- Rabbits live in groups of burrows called **warrens**.

- The hare, a cousin of the rabbit, makes a hollow in the sand called a **form**.

- A fox's hole is called his **earth**.

- Beavers live in **lodges** behind their dams.

- Your grandmother might live in a **condo-minium**.

- A badger's underground home is called a **sett**.

- Ants live in **hills**.

- Birds, wasps, and some fish build **nests**.

- Bees live in **hives**.

MODERN CREATURES THAT WERE HERE WHEN DINOSAURS ROAMED THE EARTH— OR BEFORE!

- **Algae** showed up on the scene 3½ billion years ago, along with **bacteria** and **jellyfish**.
- **Starfish** have been around for 430 million years.
- **Moss** has been gathering for 420 million years.
- **Sharks** have been biting for 375 million years.
- **Dragonflies** came around some 360 million years ago.

- **Cockroaches** showed up 350 million years ago.
- **Turtles** and **tortoises** started crawling around Earth 300 million years ago.
- **Moths** have been fluttering around for 140 million years.
- **Wild roses** began beautifying the planet 115 million years ago.

We can learn about the evolution of plants and animals over millions of years by looking at *fossils*, which are traces of living things embedded in the Earth's crust. Most fossils are either the hardened remains of plants or animals—like bones, teeth, or wood—or rocks that contain their imprints. You may have seen a necklace made of amber—the clear, hardened sap of an ancient evergreen tree. Some pieces of amber contain the remains of insects many millions of years old; they're fossils, too.

Fossils develop when plants or animals are buried in mud or sand that later hardens into rock. Because most fossils are formed in sedimentary (layered) rock, older fossils are usually found deep underground, while more recent ones are found closer to the surface. *Paleontologists*, the scientists who study fossils, can also tell how old a fossil is by testing it for elements like carbon, which decays very predictably over time. They have learned from fossils that dinosaurs flourished 250 million years ago and died out around 65 million years ago. They also know that *hominids*, man's ancestors, didn't show up until fairly recently—only about two million years ago.

FACT: If you crammed the entire history of life on earth into twenty-four hours—a single day—humans would not appear until one minute before midnight, and they would not begin to record their history until ¼ of a second before the clock struck twelve!

HEY BIG GUY!

Enormous Living Things

- The **male giraffe** is the tallest animal on Earth and grows to nearly 19 feet tall.

- The **giant squid**, which is Earth's largest invertebrate (a creature with no backbone), can reach 57 feet long.

- The **whale shark** can grow to be a menacing 40 feet long.

- The **Japanese spider crab** measures 9 feet from claw to claw.

- The **saguaro cactus** can grow to 58 feet high.

- The **Anaconda boa** can measure 37 feet long.

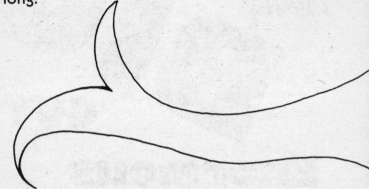

- The **FEMALE BLUE WHALE** checks in at 200 tons and is 100 feet long.

- The **male African elephant**, which is the biggest land animal on Earth, can weigh 13½ tons, and can grow to 13 feet tall.

- **Giant kelp seaweed** can grow 18 inches a day to a total length of nearly 200 feet.

- The **giant clam** can be up to 5 feet long and weigh 500 pounds.

The **female blue whale** is the largest animal that has ever lived. She's larger than the biggest dinosaur, the Brachiosaurus, which weighed only about 85 tons and was a mere 75 feet long. She is also the fastest growing animal; her fertilized egg weighs a few ten-thousandths of an ounce, but when the calf is born about 11 months later, it weighs *two tons*, and gains 200 pounds a day until it's a year old! The adult blue whale spends the summer near the North or South Pole and every day consumes *three million calories'* worth of plankton and shrimp-like creatures called krill. It spends the winter in warmer waters closer to the equator. The blues make sounds underwater to communicate with other whales and to locate food. The blue whale was once hunted for its valuable blubber and oil, but now it is a protected species.

What's the biggest animal you have ever seen?

ALL IN THE

FAMILY:
Strange Sets of Relatives

- **Grapes** and **pumpkins** are both berries.

- **SIAMESE TWINS**

- **Diamonds** and **coal** are different forms of the element carbon.

- Biologists group **rhinoceroses** and **horses** together because they are odd-toed hoofed mammals.

- **Pigs** and **camels** are even-toed hoofed mammals.

About one in every 90 human pregnancies produces twins—two babies instead of one. Twins are most often *fraternal*, meaning that they are formed from two separate fertilized eggs, and they are no more closely related than any other two siblings. But sometimes, twins are *identical*. That means that a single egg fertilized by a single sperm split and formed two identical embryos. The resulting babies have exactly the same genetic makeup.

Rarer are **Siamese twins**, identical twins who don't separate entirely during the time that they're inside their mother. They are born connected to each other, usually somewhere along the torso or at the head.

The term "Siamese twins" comes from a famous pair of twin brothers, Chang and Eng, who were born in Siam (now called Thailand) of Chinese parents in 1811. Connected at the chest, the brothers were lucky to survive. They each married and had 22 *normal children* between them. They supported themselves and their families by traveling around the world with Barnum's circus. People paid lots of money to see this "Freak of Nature." Today, doctors are sometimes able to surgically separate Siamese twins after they're born so they can lead more normal lives.

The chances of having twins are determined by *heredity*, which is the way physical characteristics are passed down to you from your parents, grandparents, and ancestors. Find out if there are any twins in your family tree. If so, someday you might be seeing double!

- **Sugarcane, wheat, barley, rye, corn, rice,** and **oats** are all members of the grass family. So when you put sugar on your cereal in the morning, you're actually staging a family reunion!

- **Snails** and **octopuses** are *mollusks*—soft-bodied animals with tiny brains.

- **Cats** and **pandas** are distant cousins.

THE SCARIEST

PEOPLE EVER:

Horrible Humans in
Fact and Fiction

- **Dracula**

- Attila and his brother ruled the Huns, a fierce Eastern European people, until around A.D. 445. Then Attila murdered his brother so he could be the only king. **Attila the Hun** was a savage warrior whose armies conquered most of eastern and central Europe. He caused so much destruction that he was called the "scourge of God."

- **Jack the Ripper**

- According to Greek mythology, **Medea** was a princess who was also a sorceress. She married a brave hero named Jason and had two children. When Jason wanted to divorce her and marry another princess, Medea was so angry that she sent the bride-to-be a lovely robe anointed with poison that burned her to death when she put it on. To complete her revenge on Jason, Medea then killed their children.

- **Ivan the Terrible** was crowned czar of Russia in 1547. During his 37-year reign, he expanded Russia's borders, but he was a cruel and ruthless man. Ivan stole his nobles' lands in a reign of terror, killed his eldest son, and murdered several of his seven wives.

- The **Wicked Witch of the West** in *The Wizard of Oz.*

- **Freddie Krueger**

- Did you ever hear this poem?

  "Lizzie Borden took an axe
  And gave her mother forty whacks.
  When she saw what she had done,
  She gave her father forty-one!"

Well, maybe she did, and then again, maybe she didn't. It's a fact that in Fall River, Massachusetts on August 4, 1892, Mr. and Mrs. Borden were hacked to death with an axe. Though Lizzie said she didn't do it, she was arrested and tried. The trial ended with a verdict of not guilty, but the case was never solved. Did Lizzie do it? We'll probably never know!

BELIEVE IT OR NOT:
Mythical Creatures— Or Are They?

- The **unicorn** is generally pictured as a beautiful white horse with a long, pointed horn growing out of the middle of its forehead. In the Middle Ages, people used to hunt the unicorn because they thought a powder made from its horn had magic powers.

- The **phoenix** was a fabulous red and gold bird that lived for 500 years, then burned itself up. A new phoenix then arose from the ashes. To the ancient Egyptians, the phoenix represented the sun, which "dies" each night and rises again each morning.

- The **Abominable Snowman**, also called the yeti, supposedly lives in the cold, snowy Himalayan Mountains. Some people who claim to have seen a yeti say that it is about seven feet tall, has huge feet, and is covered with long, thick fur.

- **Bigfoot**, whose other name is the Sasquatch, is thought to live in the Pacific Northwest of the United States, and in Canada. The Sasquatch is described as being about seven feet tall, with huge feet, and is covered with long, thick fur. (Sound familiar?)

- In the early 17th century, Norwegian fishermen believed that a humongous crab called the **kraken** lived in the ocean. It was more than a mile wide, and it looked like an island. The fisherman thought that if they landed on it, the kraken would swim down into the depths of the sea, taking them with it.

- The **griffin** first appeared in ancient Middle Eastern legends. It was a creature with the head and wings of an eagle and the body of a lion.

- In Greek mythology, a **centaur** was a creature that was half man and half horse. The horse was the bottom half, so imagine how fast a centaur could run! A centaur with a bow and arrow represents the zodiac sign Sagittarius.

- Throughout the ages, sailors have reported seeing **mermaids**, creatures that looked like beautiful women down to the waist but had fishtails instead of legs. Unlike the good little mermaid in the fairy tale, most mermaids were evil. They lured sailors to wreck their ships on the rocks.

- Some people believe that a monster lives beneath the waters of a Scottish lake called Loch Ness. The **Loch Ness Monster**, affectionately known as "Nessie," is said to look like a huge sea serpent or a dinosaur. Some people have even taken photographs that they say prove that Nessie exists!

- **Dragons** appear in myths and legends all over the world. In most countries, dragons were evil creatures that killed people, captured maidens, and destroyed towns. But in ancient China, dragons were thought to bring prosperity and good luck.

THE BIGGEST

BEETLES, BUGS, & BUTTERFLIES

- The **giant burrowing cockroach** lives in Australia. It can grow to almost four inches long and more than one inch wide. Compared to the blue whale, that's pretty tiny. But compared to a ladybug, it's *enormous*!

- The longest insect in the world is the **giant stick-insect** of Indonesia. Females have been measured up to 13 inches in body length.

- The heaviest insect is the **Goliath beetle** that lives in Equatorial Africa. A fully grown male can weigh more than three ounces and measure more than four inches long.

- Huge **dragonflies** that live in Central and South America are almost eight inches from wingtip to wingtip and nearly five inches long.

- The largest known **flea** was taken from the nest of a mountain beaver in the state of Washington almost 80 years ago. It was almost a third of an inch long. Imagine how miserable a dog would be if it had fleas that size!

- The **Queen Alexandra birdwing butterfly** of Papua New Guinea can have a wingspan of 11 inches or more.

- **Hercules moths** live in tropical Australia and New Guinea. Females can have a wingspan of more than 14 inches.

- **Millipedes** living in Africa and the Seychelles Islands can grow to more than 11 inches long. Though "millipede" means "1,000 feet," most millipedes really can have only up to 400 feet. (It's a good thing their mothers don't have to darn their socks!)

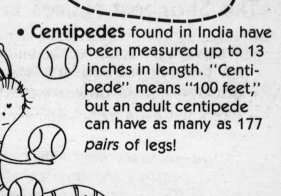

- **Centipedes** found in India have been measured up to 13 inches in length. "Centipede" means "100 feet," but an adult centipede can have as many as 177 *pairs* of legs!

FROM AARDVARK

TO ZEBU

The Strangest Names in Nature

- **Aardvark**—A South African burrowing mammal that eats ants and termites.
- **Booby**—A small, tropical water bird.
- **Cacomistle**—A tree-dwelling relative of the raccoon.
- **Drupe**—A fleshy fruit with a pit, including plums, peaches, and cherries.
- **Epizootic**—An epidemic of disease among animals.
- **Flittermouse**—An insect-eating bat that is helpful to man.

- **Geode**—A round, hollow stone lined with crystals.
- **Hornpout**—A freshwater catfish.
- **Ifkakh**—A lizard whose throat turns blue when it is excited.
- **Jackeroo**—A person who helps out on an Australian ranch.
- **Klipspringer**—A small African antelope.
- **Llama**—A South American relative of the camel.
- **Mongoose**—A small Indian mammal that eats snakes and rats.
- **No-see-ums**—Biting gnats.
- **Omnivorous**—A word describing creatures that eat both vegetables and meat.

- **Pachyderm**—A large, thick-skinned animal like the elephant or hippopotamus.

- **Quetzal**—A brightly colored Central American bird.

- **Ragwort**—A mildly poisonous relative of the daisy.

- **Sassafrass**—A North American tree whose bark is used as a flavoring and in healing.

- **Toadstool**—A poisonous mushroom.

- **Umbellifer**—A plant of the carrot family.

- **Vinegaroon**—A large, harmless scorpion that gives off a strong odor of vinegar when disturbed.

- **Warthog**—A wild African hog with large tusks and warts on its face.

- **Xylem**—The woody part of a plant stem.

- **Yak**—A longhaired Tibetan relative of the cow.

- **Zebu**—Another relative of the cow, with a big hump and long, floppy ears.

THE WORLD'S LONGEST RIVERS

River	Location	Miles
Nile	Africa	4,160
Amazon	South America	4,000
Chang Jiang (Yangtze)	China	3,964
Mississippi-Missouri-Red River	North America	3,710
Ob-Irtysh	U.S.S.R.	3,362
Huang He	China	2,903
Zaire	Africa	2,900
Amur	Asia	2,744
Lena	U.S.S.R.	2,734
Mackenzie	Canada	2,635
Mekong	Asia	2,600
Niger	Africa	2,590

BRAVE NEW

WORLDS—

Famous Voyages of Discovery

- Around the year 1000, a bold Viking named **Leif Ericsson** and his men crossed the Atlantic in their dragon-shaped boats and landed in North America. But his discovery was soon forgotten, and the continent remained unknown for almost 500 years.

- Between 1803 and 1806, **Meriwether Lewis** and **William Clark** explored the vast tract of the western United States called the Louisiana Purchase, and discovered a land route to the Pacific Ocean.

- **Christopher Columbus** set sail in 1492 with his three ships, the *Nina*, the *Pinta*, and the *Santa Maria*, in search of an eastern water route to India. His voyage was sponsored by Queen Isabella of Spain. When Columbus and his men finally reached the islands we know today as the Bahamas, they thought they had found India, so they called the natives who greeted them "Indians." Columbus' discovery of America opened a new continent to European trade and settlement, but this "new world" wasn't named after Columbus. Instead, it became known as America, after another explorer, Amerigo Vespucci.

- In 1767, **Captain James Cook** discovered Australia while exploring the South Pacific.

- The Portuguese explorer **Vasco da Gama** discovered a sea route to India in 1497. He sailed south and traveled around the tip of Africa, reaching India's western coast in 1498 and returning to Portugal in 1499, a distance of nearly 24,000 nautical miles.

- Scottish missionary **Dr. David Livingstone** explored the jungles of Africa from 1841 to 1873. While searching for the source of the Nile River, he disappeared for many years. In 1871, he was found by Henry M. Stanley, an American newspaperman. Stanley's greeting to the explorer, "Dr. Livingstone, I presume?" soon became famous.

- In 1911, **Roald Amundsen,** a Norwegian, was the first person to reach the South Pole.

- **Robert E. Peary,** an American arctic explorer, discovered the North Pole in 1909.

- In 1271, young **Marco Polo** set out from Venice, Italy with his father and uncle on an expedition to the Orient. They spent almost 20 years in China, and when they returned to Europe, nobody believed the marvelous stories they told about the splendors they had found at the court of the emperor Kublai Khan. Years later, Marco Polo published a book about his adventures. *The Book of the Travels of Marco Polo* became world famous, and may have inspired Christopher Columbus to set out on his own travels.

- On July 26, 1969, **Neil Armstrong** became the first man to set foot on the moon. As he stepped down from the lunar module, people all over the world saw him on television and heard him say, "That's one small step for man, one giant leap for mankind." **Buzz Aldrin** accompanied Armstrong on his walk, while **Michael Collins** orbited the moon in the Apollo space craft.

TEN NATURAL
WONDERS OF THE WORLD

- Victoria Falls on the border between Rhodesia and Zambia in Africa

- Grand Canyon of the Colorado River

- Great Barrier Reef of Australia, the world's largest coral reef

- Crater Lake and Wizard Island in Oregon

- Mount Everest on the Nepal–Tibet border

- Caves in France and Spain with their prehistoric paintings

- Carlsbad Caverns of New Mexico

- Giant sequoia trees of California

- Rainbow Natural Bridge of Utah

- Yellowstone Falls in Yellowstone National Park

IT'S YOUR PLANET—HELP PROTECT IT!

If you didn't realize it before, by now you know that our world is chock full of wonders. But unless we take better care of this fragile planet, one day there might not be any wonders left. Today, many rare, endangered plants and animals are protected by law. Companies and communities are being forced to stop polluting the air and water and to recycle their waste. In tropical countries, conservation groups are working to save the rainforests, which are being destroyed at the rate of 50 acres a minute. And scientists all over the world are searching for new sources of energy, like water and sunlight, that are cleaner, cheaper, and more plentiful than coal and oil.

You may not think one person can do very much to protect the environment. But our Earth needs all the help it can get, including yours. Here are some things you can do:

- Recycle newspapers, paper bags, and other waste paper. (It takes more than 500,000 trees to supply Americans with their Sunday newspapers every week.)

- Don't buy products that are packed or served in Styrofoam containers. Styrofoam is completely non-biodegradable, so it will never, *ever* decay or dissolve, even if it's buried in a landfill for hundreds of years!

- Plant a tree.

- Don't let go of helium-filled balloons. They can float far, far away and end up in the ocean, where sea creatures gobble up the partly deflated balloons, then starve to death because the latex sticks in their throats and won't allow them to swallow real food.

- When you go to the beach or the park, bring a trash bag and pick up any litter you find. And don't be a litterbug yourself!

- Turn off the lights when you leave a room. The more electricity we use, the more energy is expended and the more industrial air pollution results, contributing to the "greenhouse effect" and acid rain.

- Take quick showers instead of long baths. (Americans use 450 *billion* gallons of water *every day!*)

- Glass bottles and jars and aluminum cans can be recycled, using much less energy than it would take to make new ones using raw materials.

- Put out food and water for birds and other wildlife, especially in winter when it's hard for them to find anything to eat or drink.

- Tell other kids and grownups, too, how important it is for us all to work together for a cleaner, greener world!

NOW IT'S YOUR TURN: MAKE UP SOME LISTS OF YOUR OWN!

Here are some ideas: **MY PETS; PETS I WOULD LIKE TO HAVE; MY FAVORITE FOODS; FOODS I HATE; THE FUNNIEST PEOPLE IN THE WORLD; MY FAVORITE FLOWERS; THE BIGGEST ANIMALS I HAVE EVER SEEN; THE SMALLEST ANIMALS I HAVE EVER SEEN.** Use your imagination, and have fun!

My List: _____

_____

_____

_____

_____

_____

_____

_____

_____